THIS PLANNER
BELONGS TO:

NAME: _____

ADDRESS: _____

EMAIL: _____

PHONE: _____

2023 CALENDAR

JANUARY

S	M	T	W	T	F	S
1	2	3	4	5	6	7
8	9	10	11	12	13	14
15	16	17	18	19	20	21
22	23	24	25	26	27	28
29	30	31	1	2	3	4
5	6	7	8	9	10	11

FEBRUARY

S	M	T	W	T	F	S
29	30	31	1	2	3	4
5	6	7	8	9	10	11
12	13	14	15	16	17	18
19	20	21	22	23	24	25
26	27	28	1	2	3	4
5	6	7	8	9	10	11

MARCH

S	M	T	W	T	F	S
26	27	28	1	2	3	4
5	6	7	8	9	10	11
12	13	14	15	16	17	18
19	20	21	22	23	24	25
26	27	28	29	30	31	1
2	3	4	5	6	7	8

APRIL

S	M	T	W	T	F	S
26	27	28	29	30	31	1
2	3	4	5	6	7	8
9	10	11	12	13	14	15
16	17	18	19	20	21	22
23	24	25	26	27	28	29
30	1	2	3	4	5	6

MAY

S	M	T	W	T	F	S
30	1	2	3	4	5	6
7	8	9	10	11	12	13
14	15	16	17	18	19	20
21	22	23	24	25	26	27
28	29	30	31	1	2	3
4	5	6	7	8	9	10

JUNE

S	M	T	W	T	F	S
28	29	30	31	1	2	3
4	5	6	7	8	9	10
11	12	13	14	15	16	17
18	19	20	21	22	23	24
25	26	27	28	29	30	1
2	3	4	5	6	7	8

NOTES:

2023 CALENDAR

JULY

S	M	T	W	T	F	S
25	26	27	28	29	30	1
2	3	4	5	6	7	8
9	10	11	12	13	14	15
16	17	18	19	20	21	22
23	24	25	26	27	28	29
30	31	1	2	3	4	5

AUGUST

S	M	T	W	T	F	S
30	31	1	2	3	4	5
6	7	8	9	10	11	12
13	14	15	16	17	18	19
20	21	22	23	24	25	26
27	28	29	30	31	1	2
3	4	5	6	7	8	9

SEPTEMBER

S	M	T	W	T	F	S
27	28	29	30	31	1	2
3	4	5	6	7	8	9
10	11	12	13	14	15	16
17	18	19	20	21	22	23
24	25	26	27	28	29	30
1	2	3	4	5	6	7

OCTOBER

S	M	T	W	T	F	S
1	2	3	4	5	6	7
8	9	10	11	12	13	14
15	16	17	18	19	20	21
22	23	24	25	26	27	28
29	30	31	1	2	3	4
5	6	7	8	9	10	11

NOVEMBER

S	M	T	W	T	F	S
29	30	31	1	2	3	4
5	6	7	8	9	10	11
12	13	14	15	16	17	18
19	20	21	22	23	24	25
26	27	28	29	30	1	2
3	4	5	6	7	8	9

DECEMBER

S	M	T	W	T	F	S
26	27	28	29	30	1	2
3	4	5	6	7	8	9
10	11	12	13	14	15	16
17	18	19	20	21	22	23
24	25	26	27	28	29	30
31	1	2	3	4	5	6

NOTES:

VISION BOARD

VISION BOARD

2023 YEAR PLANNER

JAN	FEB	MAR	APR	MAY	JUN
1	1	1	1	1	1
2	2	2	2	2	2
3	3	3	3	3	3
4	4	4	4	4	4
5	5	5	5	5	5
6	6	6	6	6	6
7	7	7	7	7	7
8	8	8	8	8	8
9	9	9	9	9	9
10	10	10	10	10	10
11	11	11	11	11	11
12	12	12	12	12	12
13	13	13	13	13	13
14	14	14	14	14	14
15	15	15	15	15	15
16	16	16	16	16	16
17	17	17	17	17	17
18	18	18	18	18	18
19	19	19	19	19	19
20	20	20	20	20	20
21	21	21	21	21	21
22	22	22	22	22	22
23	23	23	23	23	23
24	24	24	24	24	24
25	25	25	25	25	25
26	26	26	26	26	26
27	27	27	27	27	27
28	28	28	28	28	28
29		29	29	29	29
30		30	30	30	30
31		31		31	

2023 YEAR PLANNER

JUL	AUG	SEP	OCT	NOV	DEC
	1	1	1	1	1
2	2	2	2	2	2
3	3	3	3	3	3
4	4	4	4	4	4
5	5	5	5	5	5
6	6	6	6	6	6
7	7	7	7	7	7
8	8	8	8	8	8
9	9	9	9	9	9
10	10	10	10	10	10
11	11	11	11	11	11
12	12	12	12	12	12
13	13	13	13	13	13
14	14	14	14	14	14
15	15	15	15	15	15
16	16	16	16	16	16
17	17	17	17	17	17
18	18	18	18	18	18
19	19	19	19	19	19
20	20	20	20	20	20
21	21	21	21	21	21
22	22	22	22	22	22
23	23	23	23	23	23
24	24	24	24	24	24
25	25	25	25	25	25
26	26	26	26	26	26
27	27	27	27	27	27
28	28	28	28	28	28
29	29	29	29	29	29
30	30	30	30	30	30
31	31		31		31

JANUARY

SUNDAY	MONDAY	TUESDAY	WEDNESDAY
1	2	3	4
8	9	10	11
15	16	17	18
22	23	24	25
29	30	31	

THURSDAY	FRIDAY	SATURDAY	NOTES
5	6	7	
12	13	14	
19	20	21	
26	27	28	

TO DO LIST

☐
☐
☐
☐
☐
☐
☐
☐
☐
☐
☐
☐
☐
☐

FEBRUARY

SUNDAY	MONDAY	TUESDAY	WEDNESDAY
			1
5	6	7	8
12	13	14	15
19	20	21	22
26	27	28	

THURSDAY	FRIDAY	SATURDAY	NOTES
	3	4	
9	10	11	
6	17	18	
23	24	25	

TO DO LIST

- ☐
- ☐
- ☐
- ☐
- ☐
- ☐
- ☐
- ☐
- ☐
- ☐
- ☐
- ☐
- ☐
- ☐

MARCH

SUNDAY	MONDAY	TUESDAY	WEDNESDAY
			1
5	6	7	8
12	13	14	15
19	20	21	22
26	27	28	29

2023

THURSDAY	FRIDAY	SATURDAY	NOTES
2	3	4	
9	10	11	
16	17	18	
23	24	25	
30	31		

TO DO LIST

- ☐
- ☐
- ☐
- ☐
- ☐
- ☐
- ☐
- ☐
- ☐
- ☐
- ☐
- ☐
- ☐

APRIL

SUNDAY	MONDAY	TUESDAY	WEDNESDAY
2	3	4	5
9	10	11	12
16	17	18	19
23	24	25	26
30			

THURSDAY	FRIDAY	SATURDAY	NOTES
		1	
6	7	8	
13	14	15	
20	21	22	
27	28	29	

TO DO LIST

- ☐
- ☐
- ☐
- ☐
- ☐
- ☐
- ☐
- ☐
- ☐
- ☐
- ☐
- ☐
- ☐
- ☐

MAY

SUNDAY	MONDAY	TUESDAY	WEDNESDAY
	1	2	3
7	8	9	10
14	15	16	17
21	22	23	24
28	29	30	31

THURSDAY	FRIDAY	SATURDAY	NOTES
4	5	6	
1	12	13	
8	19	20	
25	26	27	

TO DO LIST

- [ ]
- [ ]
- [ ]
- [ ]
- [ ]
- [ ]
- [ ]
- [ ]
- [ ]
- [ ]
- [ ]
- [ ]
- [ ]
- [ ]

JUNE

SUNDAY	MONDAY	TUESDAY	WEDNESDAY
4	5	6	7
11	12	13	14
18	19	20	21
25	26	27	28

THURSDAY	FRIDAY	SATURDAY	NOTES
	2	3	
3	9	10	
15	16	17	
22	23	24	
29	30		

TO DO LIST

☐
☐
☐
☐
☐
☐
☐
☐
☐
☐
☐
☐
☐
☐

JULY

SUNDAY	MONDAY	TUESDAY	WEDNESDAY
2	3	4	5
9	10	11	12
16	17	18	19
23	24	25	26
30	31		

THURSDAY	FRIDAY	SATURDAY	NOTES
		1	
6	7	8	
13	14	15	
20	21	22	
27	28	29	

TO DO LIST

- [ ]
- [ ]
- [ ]
- [ ]
- [ ]
- [ ]
- [ ]
- [ ]
- [ ]
- [ ]
- [ ]
- [ ]
- [ ]
- [ ]

AUGUST

SUNDAY	MONDAY	TUESDAY	WEDNESDAY
		1	2
6	7	8	9
13	14	15	16
20	21	22	23
27	28	29	30

2023

THURSDAY	FRIDAY	SATURDAY	NOTES
	4	5	
0	11	12	
7	18	19	
24	25	26	
31			

TO DO LIST

- ☐
- ☐
- ☐
- ☐
- ☐
- ☐
- ☐
- ☐
- ☐
- ☐
- ☐
- ☐
- ☐
- ☐

SEPTEMBER

SUNDAY	MONDAY	TUESDAY	WEDNESDAY
3	4	5	6
10	11	12	13
17	18	19	20
24	25	26	27

2023

THURSDAY	FRIDAY	SATURDAY	NOTES
	1	2	
7	8	9	
4	15	16	**TO DO LIST**
21	22	23	☐
28	29	30	☐

TO DO LIST

☐
☐
☐
☐
☐
☐
☐
☐
☐
☐
☐
☐
☐
☐

OCTOBER

SUNDAY	MONDAY	TUESDAY	WEDNESDAY
1	2	3	4
8	9	10	11
15	16	17	18
22	23	24	25
29	30	31	

THURSDAY	FRIDAY	SATURDAY	NOTES
	6	7	
2	13	14	
9	20	21	
26	27	28	

TO DO LIST

- ☐
- ☐
- ☐
- ☐
- ☐
- ☐
- ☐
- ☐
- ☐
- ☐
- ☐
- ☐
- ☐

NOVEMBER

SUNDAY	MONDAY	TUESDAY	WEDNESDAY
			1
5	6	7	8
12	13	14	15
19	20	21	22
26	27	28	29

THURSDAY	FRIDAY	SATURDAY	NOTES
2	3	4	
9	10	11	
16	17	18	
23	24	25	
30			

TO DO LIST

- ☐
- ☐
- ☐
- ☐
- ☐
- ☐
- ☐
- ☐
- ☐
- ☐
- ☐
- ☐
- ☐
- ☐

DECEMBER

SUNDAY	MONDAY	TUESDAY	WEDNESDAY
3	4	5	6
10	11	12	13
17	18	19	20
24	25	26	27
31			

THURSDAY	FRIDAY	SATURDAY	NOTES
	1	2	
7	8	9	
14	15	16	**TO DO LIST**
21	22	23	☐ ☐ ☐ ☐ ☐ ☐ ☐ ☐
28	29	30	☐ ☐ ☐ ☐ ☐ ☐

2024 CALENDAR

JANUARY

S	M	T	W	T	F	S
31	1	2	3	4	5	6
7	8	9	10	11	12	13
14	15	16	17	18	19	20
21	22	23	24	25	26	27
28	29	30	31	1	2	3
4	5	6	7	8	9	10

FEBRUARY

S	M	T	W	T	F	S
28	29	30	31	1	2	3
4	5	6	7	8	9	10
11	12	13	14	15	16	17
18	19	20	21	22	23	24
25	26	27	28	29	1	2
3	4	5	6	7	8	9

MARCH

S	M	T	W	T	F	S
25	26	27	28	29	1	2
3	4	5	6	7	8	9
10	11	12	13	14	15	16
17	18	19	20	21	22	23
24	25	26	27	28	29	30
31	1	2	3	4	5	6

APRIL

S	M	T	W	T	F	S
31	1	2	3	4	5	6
7	8	9	10	11	12	13
14	15	16	17	18	19	20
21	22	23	24	25	26	27
28	29	30	1	2	3	4
5	6	7	8	9	10	11

MAY

S	M	T	W	T	F	S
28	29	30	1	2	3	4
5	6	7	8	9	10	11
12	13	14	15	16	17	18
19	20	21	22	23	24	25
26	27	28	29	30	31	1
2	3	4	5	6	7	8

JUNE

S	M	T	W	T	F	S
26	27	28	29	30	31	1
2	3	4	5	6	7	8
9	10	11	12	13	14	15
16	17	18	19	20	21	22
23	24	25	26	27	28	29
30	1	2	3	4	5	6

NOTES:

2024 CALENDAR

JULY

S	M	T	W	T	F	S
30	1	2	3	4	5	6
7	8	9	10	11	12	13
14	15	16	17	18	19	20
21	22	23	24	25	26	27
28	29	30	31	1	2	3
4	5	6	7	8	9	10

AUGUST

S	M	T	W	T	F	S
28	29	30	31	1	2	3
4	5	6	7	8	9	10
11	12	13	14	15	16	17
18	19	20	21	22	23	24
25	26	27	28	29	30	31
1	2	3	4	5	6	7

SEPTEMBER

S	M	T	W	T	F	S
1	2	3	4	5	6	7
8	9	10	11	12	13	14
15	16	17	18	19	20	21
22	23	24	25	26	27	28
29	30	1	2	3	4	5
6	7	8	9	10	11	12

OCTOBER

S	M	T	W	T	F	S
29	30	1	2	3	4	5
6	7	8	9	10	11	12
13	14	15	16	17	18	19
20	21	22	23	24	25	26
27	28	29	30	31	1	2
3	4	5	6	7	8	9

NOVEMBER

S	M	T	W	T	F	S
27	28	29	30	31	1	2
3	4	5	6	7	8	9
10	11	12	13	14	15	16
17	18	19	20	21	22	23
24	25	26	27	28	29	30
1	2	3	4	5	6	7

DECEMBER

S	M	T	W	T	F	S
1	2	3	4	5	6	7
8	9	10	11	12	13	14
15	16	17	18	19	20	21
22	23	24	25	26	27	28
29	30	31	1	2	3	4
5	6	7	8	9	10	11

NOTES:

VISION BOARD

VISION BOARD

2024 YEAR PLANNER

JAN	FEB	MAR	APR	MAY	JUN
1	1	1	1	1	1
2	2	2	2	2	2
3	3	3	3	3	3
4	4	4	4	4	4
5	5	5	5	5	5
6	6	6	6	6	6
7	7	7	7	7	7
8	8	8	8	8	8
9	9	9	9	9	9
10	10	10	10	10	10
11	11	11	11	11	11
12	12	12	12	12	12
13	13	13	13	13	13
14	14	14	14	14	14
15	15	15	15	15	15
16	16	16	16	16	16
17	17	17	17	17	17
18	18	18	18	18	18
19	19	19	19	19	19
20	20	20	20	20	20
21	21	21	21	21	21
22	22	22	22	22	22
23	23	23	23	23	23
24	24	24	24	24	24
25	25	25	25	25	25
26	26	26	26	26	26
27	27	27	27	27	27
28	28	28	28	28	28
29	29	29	29	29	29
30		30	30	30	30
31		31		31	

2024 YEAR PLANNER

JUL	AUG	SEP	OCT	NOV	DEC
1	1	1	1	1	1
2	2	2	2	2	2
3	3	3	3	3	3
4	4	4	4	4	4
5	5	5	5	5	5
6	6	6	6	6	6
7	7	7	7	7	7
8	8	8	8	8	8
9	9	9	9	9	9
10	10	10	10	10	10
11	11	11	11	11	11
12	12	12	12	12	12
13	13	13	13	13	13
14	14	14	14	14	14
15	15	15	15	15	15
16	16	16	16	16	16
17	17	17	17	17	17
18	18	18	18	18	18
19	19	19	19	19	19
20	20	20	20	20	20
21	21	21	21	21	21
22	22	22	22	22	22
23	23	23	23	23	23
24	24	24	24	24	24
25	25	25	25	25	25
26	26	26	26	26	26
27	27	27	27	27	27
28	28	28	28	28	28
29	29	29	29	29	29
30	30	30	30	30	30
31	31		31		31

JANUARY

SUNDAY	MONDAY	TUESDAY	WEDNESDAY
	1	2	3
7	8	9	10
14	15	16	17
21	22	23	24
28	29	30	31

THURSDAY	FRIDAY	SATURDAY	NOTES
4	5	6	
11	12	13	
18	19	20	
25	26	27	

TO DO LIST

- ☐
- ☐
- ☐
- ☐
- ☐
- ☐
- ☐
- ☐
- ☐
- ☐
- ☐
- ☐
- ☐
- ☐

FEBRUARY

SUNDAY	MONDAY	TUESDAY	WEDNESDAY
4	5	6	7
11	12	13	14
18	19	20	21
25	26	27	28

THURSDAY	FRIDAY	SATURDAY	NOTES
1	2	3	
8	9	10	
15	16	17	
22	23	24	
29			

TO DO LIST

- ☐
- ☐
- ☐
- ☐
- ☐
- ☐
- ☐
- ☐
- ☐
- ☐
- ☐
- ☐
- ☐
- ☐

MARCH

SUNDAY	MONDAY	TUESDAY	WEDNESDAY
3	4	5	6
10	11	12	13
17	18	19	20
24	25	26	27
31			

2024

THURSDAY	FRIDAY	SATURDAY	NOTES
	1	2	
7	8	9	
14	15	16	
21	22	23	
28	29	30	

TO DO LIST

- ☐
- ☐
- ☐
- ☐
- ☐
- ☐
- ☐
- ☐
- ☐
- ☐
- ☐
- ☐
- ☐
- ☐

APRIL

SUNDAY	MONDAY	TUESDAY	WEDNESDAY
	1	2	3
7	8	9	10
14	15	16	17
21	22	23	24
28	29	30	

THURSDAY	FRIDAY	SATURDAY	NOTES
4	5	6	
11	12	13	
18	19	20	**TO DO LIST**
25	26	27	☐
			☐

TO DO LIST

☐
☐
☐
☐
☐
☐
☐
☐
☐
☐
☐
☐
☐
☐

MAY

SUNDAY	MONDAY	TUESDAY	WEDNESDAY
			1
5	6	7	8
12	13	14	15
19	20	21	22
26	27	28	29

2024

THURSDAY	FRIDAY	SATURDAY	NOTES
2	3	4	
9	10	11	
16	17	18	
23	24	25	
30	31		

TO DO LIST

- ☐
- ☐
- ☐
- ☐
- ☐
- ☐
- ☐
- ☐
- ☐
- ☐
- ☐
- ☐
- ☐
- ☐

JUNE

SUNDAY	MONDAY	TUESDAY	WEDNESDAY
2	3	4	5
9	10	11	12
16	17	18	19
23	24	25	26
30			

THURSDAY	FRIDAY	SATURDAY	NOTES
		1	
6	7	8	
13	14	15	
20	21	22	**TO DO LIST** ☐ ☐ ☐ ☐ ☐ ☐ ☐ ☐
27	28	29	☐ ☐ ☐ ☐ ☐ ☐

JULY

SUNDAY	MONDAY	TUESDAY	WEDNESDAY
	1	2	3
7	8	9	10
14	15	16	17
21	22	23	24
28	29	30	31

THURSDAY	FRIDAY	SATURDAY	NOTES
4	5	6	
11	12	13	
18	19	20	
25	26	27	

TO DO LIST

- ☐
- ☐
- ☐
- ☐
- ☐
- ☐
- ☐
- ☐
- ☐
- ☐
- ☐
- ☐
- ☐
- ☐

AUGUST

SUNDAY	MONDAY	TUESDAY	WEDNESDAY
4	5	6	7
11	12	13	14
18	19	20	21
25	26	27	28

2024

THURSDAY	FRIDAY	SATURDAY	NOTES
1	2	3	
8	9	10	
15	16	17	
22	23	24	
29	30	31	

TO DO LIST

- ☐
- ☐
- ☐
- ☐
- ☐
- ☐
- ☐
- ☐
- ☐
- ☐
- ☐
- ☐
- ☐
- ☐

SEPTEMBER

SUNDAY	MONDAY	TUESDAY	WEDNESDAY
1	2	3	4
8	9	10	11
15	16	17	18
22	23	24	25
29	30		

THURSDAY	FRIDAY	SATURDAY	NOTES
5	6	7	
12	13	14	
19	20	21	**TO DO LIST**
26	27	28	☐ ☐ ☐ ☐ ☐ ☐ ☐ ☐
			☐ ☐ ☐ ☐ ☐ ☐

OCTOBER

SUNDAY	MONDAY	TUESDAY	WEDNESDAY
		1	2
6	7	8	9
13	14	15	16
20	21	22	23
27	28	29	30

2024

THURSDAY	FRIDAY	SATURDAY	NOTES
3	4	5	
10	11	12	
17	18	19	
24	25	26	
31			

TO DO LIST

- ☐
- ☐
- ☐
- ☐
- ☐
- ☐
- ☐
- ☐
- ☐
- ☐
- ☐
- ☐
- ☐
- ☐

NOVEMBER

SUNDAY	MONDAY	TUESDAY	WEDNESDAY
3	4	5	6
10	11	12	13
17	18	19	20
24	25	26	27

THURSDAY	FRIDAY	SATURDAY	NOTES
	1	2	
7	8	9	
14	15	16	
21	22	23	
28	29	30	

TO DO LIST

- ☐
- ☐
- ☐
- ☐
- ☐
- ☐
- ☐
- ☐
- ☐
- ☐
- ☐
- ☐
- ☐
- ☐

DECEMBER

SUNDAY	MONDAY	TUESDAY	WEDNESDAY
1	2	3	4
8	9	10	11
15	16	17	18
22	23	24	25
29	30	31	

THURSDAY	FRIDAY	SATURDAY	NOTES
5	6	7	
12	13	14	
19	20	21	
26	27	28	

TO DO LIST

- ☐
- ☐
- ☐
- ☐
- ☐
- ☐
- ☐
- ☐
- ☐
- ☐
- ☐
- ☐
- ☐
- ☐

PASSWORD LOG

Website:

Username:

Password:

Notes:

Website:

Username:

Password:

Notes:

Website:

Username:

Password:

Notes:

Website:

Username:

Password:

Notes:

Website:

Username:

Password:

Notes:

Website:

Username:

Password:

Notes:

Website:

Username:

Password:

Notes:

Website:

Username:

Password:

Notes:

Website:

Username:

Password:

Notes:

Website:

Username:

Password:

Notes:

PASSWORD LOG

Website:	Website:
Username:	Username:
Password:	Password:
Notes:	Notes:

Website:	Website:
Username:	Username:
Password:	Password:
Notes:	Notes:

Website:	Website:
Username:	Username:
Password:	Password:
Notes:	Notes:

Website:	Website:
Username:	Username:
Password:	Password:
Notes:	Notes:

Website:	Website:
Username:	Username:
Password:	Password:
Notes:	Notes:

PASSWORD LOG

Website:

Username:

Password:

Notes:

Website:

Username:

Password:

Notes:

Website:

Username:

Password:

Notes:

Website:

Username:

Password:

Notes:

Website:

Username:

Password:

Notes:

Website:

Username:

Password:

Notes:

Website:

Username:

Password:

Notes:

Website:

Username:

Password:

Notes:

Website:

Username:

Password:

Notes:

Website:

Username:

Password:

Notes:

PASSWORD LOG

Website:

Username:

Password:

Notes:

Website:

Username:

Password:

Notes:

Website:

Username:

Password:

Notes:

Website:

Username:

Password:

Notes:

Website:

Username:

Password:

Notes:

Website:

Username:

Password:

Notes:

Website:

Username:

Password:

Notes:

Website:

Username:

Password:

Notes:

Website:

Username:

Password:

Notes:

Website:

Username:

Password:

Notes:

CONTACT NAMES

Name:

Phone:

Email:

Address:

Name:

Phone:

Email:

Address:

Name:

Phone:

Email:

Address:

Name:

Phone:

Email:

Address:

Name:

Phone:

Email:

Address:

Name:

Phone:

Email:

Address:

Name:

Phone:

Email:

Address:

Name:

Phone:

Email:

Address:

Name:

Phone:

Email:

Address:

Name:

Phone:

Email:

Address:

CONTACT NAMES

Name:

Phone:

Email:

Address:

Name:

Phone:

Email:

Address:

Name:

Phone:

Email:

Address:

Name:

Phone:

Email:

Address:

Name:

Phone:

Email:

Address:

Name:

Phone:

Email:

Address:

Name:

Phone:

Email:

Address:

Name:

Phone:

Email:

Address:

Name:

Phone:

Email:

Address:

Name:

Phone:

Email:

Address:

CONTACT NAMES

Name:	**Name:**
Phone:	**Phone:**
Email:	**Email:**
Address:	**Address:**

Name:	**Name:**
Phone:	**Phone:**
Email:	**Email:**
Address:	**Address:**

Name:	**Name:**
Phone:	**Phone:**
Email:	**Email:**
Address:	**Address:**

Name:	**Name:**
Phone:	**Phone:**
Email:	**Email:**
Address:	**Address:**

Name:	**Name:**
Phone:	**Phone:**
Email:	**Email:**
Address:	**Address:**

CONTACT NAMES

Name:	Name:
Phone:	Phone:
Email:	Email:
Address:	Address:

Name:	Name:
Phone:	Phone:
Email:	Email:
Address:	Address:

Name:	Name:
Phone:	Phone:
Email:	Email:
Address:	Address:

Name:	Name:
Phone:	Phone:
Email:	Email:
Address:	Address:

Name:	Name:
Phone:	Phone:
Email:	Email:
Address:	Address:

Made in the USA
Columbia, SC
09 January 2023

FLASH POINTS

STAND UP!

FIGHTING FOR CIVIL RIGHTS

Eleanor Cardell

Stand Up!
Flash Points

Full Tilt Press
42982 Osgood Road
Fremont, CA 94539
readfulltilt.com

Full Tilt Press publications may be purchased for educational, business, or sales promotional use.

Design and layout by Sara Radka
Copyedited by Renae Gilles

Getty Images: Alex Wong, 23, Bill Pugliano, 22, Christian Petersen, 40, iStockphoto, 48, Pete Souza/White
House Photo, 23, Stephen Shugerman, 41; Newscom: 17, 18, 20, 27, 32, 39, William C. Greene/TSN/Icon SMI,
5, Black Star, 36, EPA, 42, Everett Collection, 16, 31, NOTIMEX, 43, Picture History, 7, Sport The Library,
38, Sporting News Archives/Icon SMI, 12, TSN/Icon SMI, 7, 10, Underwood Archives, 9, 15; Shutterstock,
6, 17, 26, 26, 30, 37, 37; Wikimedia: AP, 35, Bowman Gum, 12, Frank Gatteri, United States Army Signal
Corps, 11, Harris & Ewing, 6, John Vachon, 7, Library of Congress, 25, 27, Mrsdonzaleighabernathy, 29, O.
J. Rapp, 32, Rowland Scherman, 19, Stanley Wolfson, 27, 28, State Archives of North Carolina, 21, Tawanda
Boatner Green, 16, U.S. National Archives and Records Administration, 8, Yoichi R. Okamoto, 36

ISBN: 978-1-62920-606-6 (library binding)
ISBN: 978-1-62920-618-9 (eBook)

Contents

Jackie Robinson

4

**The Montgomery
Bus Boycott**

14

**The Selma to
Montgomery March**

24

**Protest at the
1968 Olympics**

34

Quiz 44
Glossary 45
Index 46
Read More 47

JACKIE ROBINSON

April 15, 1947

Fans crowd into Ebbets Field in Brooklyn, New York. They are here to see the Brooklyn Dodgers play the Boston Braves. People crane their necks to see the players. They are looking for Jackie Robinson. He's the first African American to ever play for a Major League Baseball (MLB) team. This is his first game.

By the sixth inning, Robinson has not scored. He is not playing his best. He is nervous. He knows that a lot of people don't want him to play. Some of his teammates don't want him on the team. Many of the Braves players don't want to play against him. They yell at him. They call him names.

Robinson knows that he can't fail. If he does, people will say that African Americans don't belong in the major leagues. In the seventh inning, Robinson scores the first run of his MLB career. He helps the Dodgers win. This win means more than just a baseball game. It means progress toward **integrating** Major League Baseball.

integrate: to stop keeping people of different races apart

Jackie Robinson was Rookie of the Year in 1947. In that season, he had a batting average of .297, with 12 home runs and 48 runs batted in.

DID YOU KNOW?
April 15 of every year is Jackie Robinson Day in the major leagues. Everyone on the field wears his old number: 42.

How and Why

Historical events rarely have only one simple cause. Many different things—such as certain events or changing ways of thinking—work together to shape the future. Below are some of the things that led to Jackie Robinson's career in Major League Baseball.

From a Young Age

Robinson played a lot of sports growing up. He was always very good at them. At UCLA, Robinson played four sports at the varsity level. He also played professional football in Hawai'i.

An Unwelcoming Sport

In 1942, President Franklin D. Roosevelt said that he considered baseball to be very important. It was popular across the country. Watching baseball games helped many Americans relax and have fun. At first, major league teams didn't want to accept African American players. The organizations thought that many white fans might stop supporting the sport.

Unfair Treatment

African Americans were treated very differently from white Americans. There used to be many laws that required segregation, separating people based on their race. For example, African Americans and white Americans couldn't eat at the same restaurants, go to the same schools, or use the same restrooms.

Negro Leagues

Before 1947, baseball leagues were segregated. Robinson played in a Negro League. But there weren't any official rules that said African Americans couldn't play in the major leagues.

Integration Begins

Branch Rickey was the president of the Brooklyn Dodgers. He wanted to integrate the major leagues. Robinson seemed perfect. First he put Robinson on a minor league team, and that went well. So Rickey decided to move Robinson to the majors.

What Happened Next

Many people were upset that Robinson joined the majors. His team members were upset, too. But the Dodgers' manager supported Robinson. He didn't listen to Robinson's teammates. He said he would rather trade them away than Robinson. But the players chose to remain on the team and play with Robinson.

There were many laws in the United States that separated African Americans from white people. Often, Robinson couldn't stay in hotels with his teammates. Sometimes they couldn't eat in the same restaurants.

But many people in the United States were very excited when Robinson joined the Dodgers. Finally, an African American man was playing in the majors. Many wanted to show their support. They quickly became fans of the Brooklyn Dodgers.

Baseball was, and still is, the "American **pastime**." Robinson was put in the public spotlight when he joined the majors. At first, some Dodgers fans only saw the color of Robinson's skin. But as they watched him play baseball, they finally started to see him as a person, and a skilled player.

More fans than ever came to watch Jackie Robinson play for the Brooklyn Dodgers. During the 1947 season, the team broke attendance records at every stadium they played in.

pastime: an activity that people enjoy during their free time

DID YOU KNOW?
Jackie Robinson was awarded the Presidential Medal of Freedom after his death.

Ripple Effects

A single event, no matter how big or small it may seem at the time, can have a big impact on the future. After Jackie Robinson joined the major leagues, many important changes took place in US sports.

A Larger Goal

Robinson continued to fight against racism after he joined the majors. He wrote letters to the president. He marched in protests. He helped open a bank that welcomed African Americans. Robinson wanted to integrate schools and stop violence against African Americans.

Moving to the Majors

At first, African Americans had not been welcomed into the majors. Because of this, the first Negro League was formed in 1920. Later, after Jackie Robinson joined the major leagues, African American athletes moved to the majors instead.

Integrated Sports

Today, there are no segregated sports leagues in the United States. The National Football League integrated in 1946, the year before Major League Baseball. More than 70 percent of NFL players are now African American. The National Basketball Association integrated in 1950. Now, 75 percent of NBA players are African American.

Integrating the Military

The integration of baseball was just one small step forward in the fight for equality. President Harry S. Truman wanted to go further. He wanted to integrate the Armed Forces as well. In 1948, President Truman ordered the Armed Forces to integrate.

Jackie Robinson (left) paved the way for many other African American baseball players. Monte Irvin (right) is considered one of the best. Irvin made his debut with the New York Giants in 1949, and hit 99 home runs during his MLB career.

LARRY DOBY

After Jackie Robinson joined the major leagues, more African Americans quickly followed. The second was a man named Larry Doby. He went straight from a Negro League to the majors. Doby played for the Cleveland Indians. His first MLB game was on July 5, 1947. This was less than three months after Robinson's. Doby played for the major leagues for 13 years, and was named an All-Star player 7 times.

A Welcoming Sport

Robinson played for the Brooklyn Dodgers for nine years. People didn't think **desegregation** would work. But Robinson never backed down. He stood up against racism through his entire life. Robinson's success gave President Truman confidence. Soon, the Armed Forces were desegregated, as well. These changes gave civil rights leaders more hope. People began to believe that the whole country could be desegregated.

Before Jackie Robinson joined the Dodgers, African Americans could only play in the Negro Leagues. But after 1947, many African American athletes moved from the Negro Leagues to the majors. Their fans followed them. Major League Baseball began to attract even more fans. In 1949, the Negro National League shut down after losing many of its star players. Another Negro League, the Negro American League, lasted a few years longer. But it eventually shut down in 1962.

Before Robinson joined the majors, dark-skinned Latino players had also joined the Negro Leagues. However, once Robinson switched to the majors, Latino players began to join, too. In 1949, two years after Robinson joined the majors, the first dark-skinned Latino player played in a major league game. Now, Major League Baseball welcomes people of all races. More than 40 percent of MLB players are not white. They are African American, Latino, Asian, or of other ethnicities. Today, MLB athletes come from the US and 19 other countries around the world.

desegregation: ending a policy that keeps people of different races separate

DID YOU KNOW?
In 1962, Jackie Robinson joined the National Baseball Hall of Fame.

THE MONTGOMERY BUS BOYCOTT

December 5, 1955

The buses in Montgomery, Alabama, are quiet. Usually they are filled with people. Four days earlier, Rosa Parks was arrested for not giving up her seat for a white man. Today, many of the seats are empty.

African Americans are tired of being mistreated. When riding buses, they have to sit at the back. They have to pay the driver in the front, but get on in the back. Some buses don't stop at each corner in African American neighborhoods the way they do in white neighborhoods.

Because of this unfair treatment, African Americans have decided not to ride the buses at all. They are going to force the laws to change. Crowds walk along the sidewalks. Some ride bikes. Others pile into carpools. Almost no African Americans are riding the buses.

This is the first day of the Montgomery Bus **Boycott**.

boycott: a form of protest where people refuse to use or participate in something

Some people said that Rosa Parks refused to give up her bus seat to a white man because she was tired after a long day at work. However, Parks said she wasn't physically tired. She was "tired of giving in."

DID YOU KNOW?
Rosa Parks was given the Presidential Medal of Freedom in 1996.

How and Why

Historical events rarely have only one simple cause. Many different things—such as certain events or changing ways of thinking—work together to shape the future. Take a look at some of the things that led to the Montgomery Bus Boycott.

Peaceful Protests

Americans had been peacefully protesting inequality for many years. In the 1940s, African American students in Washington, D.C., protested against white-only restaurants. They'd sit down and refuse to leave, even though the restaurant wouldn't serve them. These protests were called sit-ins. They helped peaceful protests become more popular.

Past Success

In 1953, there was a successful bus boycott in Baton Rouge, Louisiana. It lasted two weeks. Before the protest, African Americans were only allowed to sit in the back of the bus. Afterward, African American leaders reached an agreement with the buses. Most—though not all—seats were allowed to be filled on a first-come-first-served basis.

Rosa Parks

Months before the Montgomery Bus Boycott, several African American women had been arrested. They had refused to give up their seats. Then in December, Rosa Parks, a respected civil rights activist, was arrested for the same thing. The Women's Political Council (WPC) was notified. This was a group who fought for African American civil rights. They decided to use Rosa Parks and her arrest to begin fighting segregation on the buses. Segregation means separating people based on their race. Civil rights leaders called for a bus boycott on the day of Rosa Parks's trial.

Spreading the Word

The WPC planned the boycott. They told people it would begin on December 5. Other civil rights groups started to talk about it, and African Americans spread the news through the community. Radios and newspapers picked up the story. It was all over the news. Soon, everyone knew about the boycott.

The 13-month legal battle to end segregation on buses started at the courthouse in Montgomery (pictured). It successfully ended in the Supreme Court.

DID YOU KNOW?
Ninety percent of the African American bus riders in Montgomery boycotted the buses. At the time, that was about 40,000 people.

What Happened Next

The Montgomery Bus Boycott was only supposed to last for one day. But on that day, the boycott was very successful. That night, civil rights leaders got together. They decided to form a new organization, the Montgomery Improvement Association (MIA). This group would be in charge of the boycott, which ended up lasting for more than a year. Martin Luther King Jr. was the head of the MIA.

Martin Luther King Jr. became the face and voice of the Civil Rights Movement across the United States. He gave many famous speeches. One of these is the "I Have a Dream" speech. It is one of the most well-known speeches of the Civil Rights Movement.

At first, the MIA didn't think they could end segregation on the buses with one boycott. They only wanted to improve the conditions for African American bus riders. But the boycott worked. The MIA realized that they had a lot of support. So the MIA worked to change people's minds. People began to say that it was wrong for buses to be segregated. The US Constitution didn't allow it. They wanted equal rights to ride the buses.

Ripple Effects

A single event, no matter how big or small it may seem at the time, can have a big impact on the future. The bus boycott in Montgomery led to many very important changes in the United States.

Big News

The Montgomery Bus Boycott was all over the news. More than 100 reporters visited Montgomery and reported on the boycott. Many people around the world started paying attention to the Civil Rights Movement.

Integrated Buses

The Montgomery Bus Boycott lasted for more than a year. The case went all the way to the Supreme Court. The Supreme Court ruled that segregating the buses was against the Constitution. On December 21, 1956, the buses stopped forcing travelers to divide bus seats based on race.

Further Desegregation

The Supreme Court had made it illegal to divide buses and trains based on race. But in the South, places like bus station bathrooms were still separated. In 1961, the Interstate Commerce Commission made new rules. These rules banned segregation in every place of transportation.

Successful Protests

Peaceful protests continued to succeed. In February 1960, four African American college students walked into a store called Woolworth's and ordered coffee. They were told to leave. But they came back the next day. Students across the South followed their example. More than 50,000 students were involved in sit-ins. Slowly, restaurants in the South started to integrate.

DID YOU KNOW?

Rosa Parks was given a fine of $14 for refusing to give up her seat. This would cost about $125 today.

The Movement Begins

African Americans were frustrated. They deserved the same rights as white people. When Rosa Parks was arrested, leaders saw a chance to make changes. They used Rosa Parks as the face of the movement.

The bus boycott in Montgomery was a huge success. The African-American community pulled together. People started to carpool, and others took care of children while their parents worked. The Montgomery Bus Boycott began the Civil Rights Movement. It was the first time that many people had protested together. It changed the way protests were done in the United States.

The Montgomery Bus Boycott was another step toward total integration in the United States. It also made Martin Luther King Jr. into a powerful figure. He quickly became an important civil rights leader. Today he is an **icon** of the African American Civil Rights Movement. People still listen to his powerful speeches, and continue working toward his goal of equal rights for all people.

icon: a well-known symbol

Rosa Parks's bus can be visited at the Henry Ford Museum near Detroit, Michigan. President Barack Obama sat in Parks's seat in 2012.

MAKING HISTORY

Until 2009, the United States had never had an African American President. But in 2007, a young Democratic senator from Illinois decided to run. His name was Barack Obama. His campaign was very successful, and in August 2008, he became the Democratic nominee for president. The United States was having lots of problems with the economy, and many people were unemployed. Obama promised to fix all that.

On January 8, 2009, Barack Obama became President of the United States and was the first African American to hold the office.

THE SELMA TO MONTGOMERY MARCH

March 25, 1965

People come marching into Montgomery, Alabama. Everyone is tired. It took five straight days of walking to travel from Selma to Montgomery. It was a dangerous journey. Soldiers were watching over them, but some fights still broke out. Some people were hurt. Many white people didn't want the march to reach the capitol. The marchers want to stop the fight against voter **suppression** in Alabama and much of the South. Now, the protesters pack onto the lawn in front of the Capitol Building. They hope that lawmakers are ready to hear their message.

Dr. Martin Luther King Jr. stands on the steps. He led the march from Selma to Montgomery. King begins to speak. He praises the people for marching. He tells them that they must keep fighting for civil rights because change is coming. "How long will prejudice blind the visions of men?" King asks the crowd. "Not long!"

suppression: stopping something by force

During the march to Montgomery, many people got blisters on their feet and sunburns on their faces. Dr. Martin Luther King Jr. had a blister so bad that he wasn't sure if he could finish the march.

DID YOU KNOW?

Between 25,000 and 30,000 people made the march from Selma to Montgomery.

How and Why

Historical events rarely have only one simple cause. Many different things—such as certain events or changing ways of thinking—work together to shape the future. Below are some of the events that led to the march to Montgomery.

March on Washington

In August 1963, 200,000 people marched through Washington. There, Martin Luther King Jr. delivered his speech, "I Have a Dream." After, King met with President John F. Kennedy. They started working on the Civil Rights Act of 1964. This law made it so African Americans could get jobs without being treated unfairly.

Voter Suppression

Even though the law said they were allowed to vote, many African Americans still weren't able to. Voter suppression was common in the South. Many people's right to vote was being taken away illegally. They were forced to take unfair tests and pay a large fee, called a poll tax, for local elections.

Protesting Violence

Birmingham, Alabama, was one of the most segregated cities in the South. This meant that people were separated based on race. Many people wanted it to stay that way. Violence was common. On September 15th, 1963, a church was bombed. More than 20 people were injured, and 4 young girls died. People were furious.

Bloody Sunday

To fight against voter suppression, Martin Luther King Jr. organized a march. The group left Selma on March 7, 1965, and headed to Montgomery. However, after marching through Selma, they were blocked at a bridge by state troopers. The troopers got very violent and many people were injured. That day is known as Bloody Sunday.

Protecting Protesters

On March 15, President Lyndon Johnson spoke to congress about voters' rights. He supported the march, and told Alabama that the marchers should be allowed to travel to Montgomery. But the Alabama governor said he would not protect the marchers. So President Johnson sent in US National Guard troops to keep them safe.

What Happened Next

The pictures of Bloody Sunday and the march from Selma to Montgomery made people pay attention. Police and state troopers put more than 50 people in the hospital. The rest of the US realized that voter suppression was a big problem in the South. The laws for equal rights were being ignored.

Many African American voters had to take tests before they were allowed to **register** to vote. The tests were confusing and long. One wrong answer meant they would fail. Almost nobody passed. But in August, President Johnson signed the Voting Rights Act of 1965. It got rid of the tests and other barriers. Finally, many African Americans could register to vote.

Before, the government hadn't said that there was a problem with voter suppression. But now, the president had noticed. The movement was getting more support. People were starting to understand. It looked like things might be starting to change.

register: to add your name to an official list in order to be allowed to do something

During the march from Selma to Montgomery, protesters sang many songs about freedom, hope, and love.

DID YOU KNOW?
Before the march, only 2 percent of Selma's African American population was able to register to vote.

Ripple Effects

A single event, no matter how big or small it may seem at the time, can have a big impact on the future. The historic march to Montgomery had many long-lasting effects.

Voting Rights

The Voting Rights Act of 1965 made poll taxes illegal. This made it easier for African Americans to register to vote. Right away, more than 100,000 African Americans registered to vote in Alabama.

The Power to Change

As more African Americans were able to vote, more African Americans ran for office and became elected officials. Officials have power to make legal changes. They can fight to protect civil rights from inside the government.

Equal Rights Today

The Voting Rights Act has changed since the 1960s. In the 1970s, it expanded to protect people who didn't speak English. Today, the Voting Rights Act is still working to help make voting rights equal for all people.

Fair Housing

In 1968, another civil rights law was passed. It is known as the Fair Housing Act. In the 1960s, it was hard for African Americans to find places to live. White landlords didn't want to rent to them. But the Fair Housing Act said that people couldn't refuse someone housing based on race, gender, or religion.

DID YOU KNOW?

In 2015, a movie about the march to Montgomery was released. It is called *Selma*, and was nominated for the Academy Award for Best Picture.

President Lyndon B. Johnson used more than 75 pens to sign all the pages of the Civil Rights Act in 1964. He then gave the pens away as mementos. Dr. Martin Luther King Jr. received one.

EDMUND PETTUS BRIDGE

On the day that would become known as Bloody Sunday, marchers were stopped by state troopers at the Edmund Pettus Bridge. Because of the violence that happened at the bridge, it became famous. In 2013, it was made a historic landmark. It is also part of the Selma to Montgomery National Historic Trail.

Marching for Change

The march from Selma to Montgomery changed the US forever. People saw the violence of Bloody Sunday. They saw the dedication of the marchers, who walked 12 miles a day and slept in fields. This inspired people to support and join the Civil Rights Movement. People began to create laws that have shaped the country.

Dr. Martin Luther King Jr. believed in the importance of protesting peacefully. Many others have followed his approach. In the 1960s and 1970s, thousands of people protested the Vietnam War (1954–1975). People marched against the use of nuclear energy in the 1980s. In 2011, protesters spent weeks living in a park in New York City to protest unfairness in the business world.

These protests start peacefully. But in some cases, like Bloody Sunday, protests become violent. Violence may get people's attention. But research shows that nonviolent protests get better results. Peaceful protests are an effective way to bring about change.

DID YOU KNOW?

In March 2015, President Barack Obama went to Selma to join the 50th anniversary celebration of the march.

PROTEST AT THE 1968 OLYMPICS

October 16, 1968

It is the middle of the Summer Olympic Games in Mexico City. The 200 meter run has just ended. The athletes are going to receive their medals. One, Peter Norman, is Australian. The other two are African American. Their names are Tommie Smith and John Carlos.

The United States' **national anthem** begins to play. But Smith and Carlos don't stand tall or sing. They bow their heads and raise one fist. They are both wearing one black glove. They are wearing no shoes and black socks.

The crowd goes completely silent. Nobody expected this. Smith and Carlos are making a statement about equality and civil rights. But many people think they are being disrespectful. The crowd begins to boo and shout insults. They don't believe that the Olympics is a place for political protests. Smith and Carlos brace themselves for violence. They wonder if they will be attacked. Even if they are hurt, they think that it is worth the sacrifice. They are standing up for what they believe.

national anthem: a song that is accepted as a particular country's official song

During their salute, Tommie Smith (middle) held his arm straight up. John Carlos (right) kept his angled to the side. He wanted to be able to defend himself quickly if he was attacked.

DID YOU KNOW?
Tommie Smith won gold and John Carlos won bronze in the 200 meter sprint.

How and Why

Historical events rarely have only one simple cause. Many different things—such as certain events or changing ways of thinking—work together to shape the future. Take a look at some of the things that led to Smith and Carlos's memorable protest at the 1968 Olympics.

Changing Viewpoints

In the 1950s and '60s, many new laws had been passed that helped the Civil Rights Movement. However, people were still not being treated equally. African Americans lived in poverty. White Americans mistreated them. They had trouble finding jobs and places to live.

Assassinations

The year 1968 had been filled with tragedy. Senator Robert F. Kennedy had been assassinated earlier that year. He was a politician from New York. Kennedy was a strong supporter of civil rights. Soon after, Martin Luther King Jr. was assassinated. He had been a leader of the Civil Rights Movement.

A Call for Peace

The Vietnam War had been going on for almost 10 years. Thousands of American soldiers had been sent to Vietnam and many died in combat. A lot of young people didn't like the war. They were also realizing that the laws promising equal rights were not being followed. The Civil Rights Movement and the anti-war movement began to work together and fight for peace and equality.

Olympic Boycott

African American athletes had been encouraged to boycott the 1968 Olympics. Not going to the games would send a message to the world. People wanted to make a statement about civil rights and inequality. But the boycott failed. Smith and Carlos went to the games. They decided to make their own statement there.

What Happened Next

Tommie Smith and John Carlos's raised fists, or "power fists," made the news all over the world. A lot of reporters didn't like the political statement. They wanted to report on the Olympics, not civil rights. Many people **criticized** Smith and Carlos. They believed that the two athletes had made the wrong choice.

Smith and Carlos were kicked out of the Olympics. There are strict rules about athletes not making political statements. Smith and Carlos had broken those rules. Because of this, many people turned against them. People felt that Smith and Carlos were no longer heroes.

A lot of people accused them of being anti-American. The national anthem is a source of pride to many. People said the athletes were being disrespectful because they protested during the anthem.

The African American Civil Rights Movement suddenly gained a lot more attention. Not all of it was positive. But people were talking about civil rights. They were aware of the problems Smith and Carlos had protested. The athletes had done what they had set out to do.

criticize: to express disapproval of someone or something

John Carlos said he let Tommie Smith win gold in the race. Carlos didn't think Smith would raise his fist if he came in second.

DID YOU KNOW?

Most of the world did not view Smith's and Carlos's power fists as a bad thing. It was only America that got very upset over it.

Ripple Effects

A single event, no matter how big or small it may seem at the time, can have a big impact on the future. Carlos and Smith's salute at the 1968 Olympics brought attention to an important cause, and set an example for peaceful protests in the future.

An Important Message

Smith and Carlos had protested racism. But they experienced even more racism in return. Their sports careers ended. They were banned from the Olympics. This unfair treatment was exactly what they had wanted people to be aware of.

In the Public Eye

Many sporting events are shown on TV. They are seen by millions of people. In 2010, members of the Phoenix Suns basketball team wore jerseys that said "Los Suns." Los is Spanish for "the." They mixed Spanish with their team name to protest a new law. The players felt that this law was unfair to people from Mexico.

Recent Protest

In 2016, another sports star made a very public protest. Football player Colin Kaepernick refused to stand during the US national anthem. He was protesting the unfair treatment of African Americans. He wanted to make people aware that police violence against African Americans often goes unpunished.

Remembering Heroism

Today people think about Smith and Carlos differently. They are considered heroes. Their protest at the 1968 Olympics was an important moment for the Civil Rights Movement. For their actions, both Smith and Carlos were awarded the Arthur Ashe Courage Award in 2008.

A statue capturing the historic moment of the 1968 Olympics salute can be seen in Washington, D.C., at the National Museum of African American History and Culture.

PETER NORMAN

Smith and Carlos were not the only two people on the podium that day. The third person was named Peter Norman. He was Australian. He had placed second. Smith and Carlos had told Norman what they were going to do. Norman supported them. During the Olympics, he wore a pin protesting racism. He told everyone that he agreed with Smith and Carlos. For this action, Norman's career was ruined. Nobody wanted him on their team. But he never backed down from his support of Smith and Carlos.

Symbol of Resistance

Tommie Smith and John Carlos wanted to use their moment of glory to make a lasting difference in the world. Their protest changed their own lives, and the lives of many others. Their raised fists became a symbol of the fight for equality. Today, they are called heroes and their bravery is honored.

Many events have happened since the Olympic salute that have become focal points for the Civil Rights Movement. In 2012, Trayvon Martin, a 17-year-old African American boy, was shot and killed by a man who was never punished. In the following years, multiple African Americans were killed by police. Many news sources covered these events, and lots of people started to pay attention. In response, a new movement began. It is called Black Lives Matter.

The African American Civil Rights Movement continues to use the raised fist as a symbol to this day. During the start of the 2016 football season, multiple NFL players raised their fists during the National Anthem. The raised fist is a symbol of resistance against inequality, and the fight for equal treatment.

DID YOU KNOW?

In 2016, President Barack Obama acknowledged Smith and Carlos in a talk about the Olympic Games. He called them "legendary."

Quiz

1 In what year did Jackie Robinson play his first MLB game?

1947

2 How long did Robinson play for the Brooklyn Dodgers?

Nine years

3 Before the Montgomery Bus Boycott, another successful bus boycott took place in which city?

Baton Rouge, Louisiana

4 How long did the Montgomery Bus Boycott last?

More than a year

5 How long did it take the marchers to walk from Selma to Montgomery?

Five days

6 Who did President Johnson send to protect the marchers on their way to Montgomery?

US National Guard troops

7 In 1968, who were the two Olympic medalists who raised a fist in support of equality and civil rights?

Tommie Smith and John Carlos

8 What award were Smith and Carlos given to honor their protest at the 1968 Olympics?

The Arthur Ashe Courage Award

Glossary

boycott: a form of protest where people refuse to use or participate in something

criticize: to express disapproval of someone or something

desegregation: ending a policy that keeps people of different races separate

icon: a well-known symbol

integrate: to stop keeping people of different races apart

national anthem: a song that is accepted as a particular country's official song

pastime: an activity that people enjoy during their free time

register: to add your name to an official list in order to be allowed to do something

suppression: stopping something by force

Index

Arthur Ashe Courage Award 41

Black Lives Matter 43
Bloody Sunday 27, 28, 32, 33
Brooklyn Dodgers 4, 7, 8, 9, 13

Carlos, John 34, 35, 36, 37, 38, 39, 40,
    41, 42, 43
Civil Rights Act 26, 32
Civil Rights Movement 19, 20, 22, 33,
    36, 37, 38, 41, 43

Doby, Larry 12

Kaepernick, Colin 41
King Jr., Dr. Martin Luther 19, 22,
    24, 25, 26, 27, 32, 33, 36

Major League Baseball (MLB) 4,
    12, 13

Negro Leagues 7, 10, 12, 13
Norman, Peter 34, 42

Obama, President Barack 23, 33, 43

Parks, Rosa 14, 15, 17, 21, 22, 23

Rickey, Branch 7
Robinson, Jackie 4, 5, 6, 7, 8, 9, 10,
    12, 13

Smith, Tommie 34, 35, 36, 37, 38, 39,
    40, 41, 42, 43

Truman, President Harry 11, 13

US Constitution 19, 20

Vietnam War 33, 37
Voting Rights Act 28, 30, 31

Read More

Herman, Gail. *Who Was Jackie Robinson?* New York, NY: Grosset & Dunlap, 2011.

Denenberg, Barry. *Stealing Home: The Story of Jackie Robinson.* New York, NY: Scholastic, 1990.

Bader, Bonnie. *Who Was Martin Luther King, Jr.?* New York, NY: Grosset & Dunlap, 2008.

McDonough, Yona Zeldis. *Who Was Rosa Parks?* New York, NY: Grosset & Dunlap, 2010.

Kelso, Richard. *Walking for Freedom: The Montgomery Bus Boycott.* Austin, TX: Raintree Steck-Vaughn, 1993.

Lowery, Lynda Blackmon, et al. *Turning 15 on the Road to Freedom: My Story of the 1965 Selma Voting Rights March.* New York, NY: Dial, 2015.

Rochelle, Belinda. *Witnesses to Freedom: Young People Who Fought for Civil Rights.* New York, NY: Puffin Books, 1997.

Adler, David A. *Heroes for Civil Rights.* New York, NY: Holiday House, 2008.